Papa God
&
Me

Mary Legierski

DEDICATION

This book is dedicated to Papa God.
He's been my Papa
He's been my strength

CONTENTS

ACKNOWLEDGMENTS

I would like to acknowledge the beautiful love and care shared by the Gallagher Family, and the wonderful help from Arlene Devlin. Also, a special thank you to all who encouraged me to write this book for my Papa God.

It is His work – not mine.

"Hear this! A sower went out to sow. And as he sowed, some seed fell on the path, and the birds came and ate it up. Other seed fell on rocky ground where it had little soil. It sprang up at once because the soil was not deep. And when the sun rose, it was scorched and it withered for lack of roots. Some seed fell among thorns, and the thorns grew up and choked it and it produced no grain. And some seed fell on rich soil and produced fruit. It came up and grew and yielded thirty, sixty, and a hundredfold." He added, "Whoever has ears to hear ought to hear."

Matthew 13:3-9

PLEASE WRITE A BOOK

Now as I start with - why to write a book. This all started when I went to my dear friend's 78th surprise birthday party. The party was given by her daughter and it was held in our church's meeting room. All meetings are held in this room. This room used to be the living room for the three nuns that lived with us at our parish. These lovely ladies taught our religion classes on Sunday. Our parish people were so sad when they left our parish.

Back to the party. When I walked into the room, I met this young lady, and she told me that the man she came with was a wonderful new friend. She told me she had divorced her husband eight years ago and now she had this wonderful new friend. She also told me that he really didn't know much about God. Now, it just so happened that I sat across the table from them and we could talk to one another. As time went on, I found myself telling him about my life with my God, and I told them about the beautiful gifts God had given to me. These gifts I love to share with people. As I spoke, and as time went on, I could see this young man's eyes seemed to change as he looked at me. I truly could see that he had never heard of such things God could do. After a few of these life stories, this young man said to me, "You must write a book." When the two of them got up to leave, the young man came to me and he hugged me and whispered in my ear, "PLEASE, write a book." Many other people have told me to write a book about God in my life.

This story now will start. It must begin with me as a little girl and where life has taken me for these 87 years. I know you will see, as this young man did, how God, with His great love for His children, can make such a beautiful journey for us, if we but give Him our lives. You see, that is what I did.

As I write these stories, I wonder, will you the readers, be able to believe them. It was so interesting to me to believe what our Heavenly Father can do for us. I have no credit for any of these stories. It is God's Spirit that takes over and it is just so amazing and beautiful.

MISSION

On January 23, 1986, I lost my Sweetheart. He was my love and the father of our five children. When he left me, I really didn't know what to do with this life of mine. In September, our church put on an 8-day Mission. I was anxious to go to it, and on the fifth day, a VERY lovely lady gave us a talk. All I can remember was just as she was about to finish the talk, I left the hall and ran to the church. I knelt down. Looking at Jesus, I pleaded with Him to take my life because I didn't know what to do now that my Sweetheart was gone. It was only I and Jesus. No one else was in the church. That night I went to bed and at 3 in the morning I woke up and there above me was something. And this "something" was pouring something into my heart. I could feel something going into my heart. This was really a shock to me. I never in my life had such an experience.

The next night at Mission, I kept asking people around me if they had such a strange experience following last night. No one had. There was one lady who heard me asking people and she told me I must come up to the podium and tell everyone what had happened to me last night. I told her I could NEVER stand up and talk before seventy people. She told me – just wait and they would call me up. When they did call me, I got up and walked up to the podium and out of my mouth came such words! I heard a man in the back of the room speak aloud and say, "I could listen to this lady all night!" You see, it was not me that was speaking. It was the Holy Spirit. That's who was poured into my heart that night.

The lady that called me up that night then came to me and said I should take the "Life in the Spirit" seminar. This program was being held at another church. She said she would pick me up and take me. I did just as she said, and after learning many lovely things about our Heavenly Father, His Son, and the Holy Spirit I was amazed. They laid hands on me and prayed for the release of God's Holy Spirit over me. I was given the gift of tongues that night, also. This was the start of a new life for me. The Bible came to life and so many lovely gifts came to me. You now see what our Heavenly Father can do if you open your heart to Him.

As I start the book, I just look at how I gave my life to Jesus. It was up to

Jesus now to watch me. I didn't really even KNOW Him as I should have. For forty years I went in and out of church. Did everything they told me. But I knew there was more. I found that more that night at Mission. Jesus really came to me with His Spirit full blown.

THE BEGINNING

Now I must go back and let you know about my life as a little girl and how I started on my journey of life that God had planned for me. I was born the seventh child of Bill and Anna McGowan.

My dad was a retired Army man. He was a Teddy Roosevelt Rough Rider. Dad was born in Ireland. County Cork was the place. As a very young lad, he went to Scotland to work for a man that raised horses. He learned a lot about horses. From Scotland, he went to England where he got a job on a ship. The ship came to America and he left the ship and went to Kalamazoo, Michigan. He went to school and did graduate. He had a nice Aunt in Michigan and she took good care of him. Now, as a young lad that knew a lot about horses, he joined the 7th Calvary. I knew little about my father's life, but I do know and heard he went to the Philippines. And when the Army rounded up Geronimo, Dad had an Indian scout that was a help for them. This Indian scout, as we know now, was Tom Mix. He now had a circus that traveled around the country.

Now, how I met Tom Mix. Dad and I went to our grocery store this day, and Dad received a great surprised. While we were in the grocery store, in came Tom Mix. He had parked his RV across the road from our store and came in to get supplies. When Dad saw him, and he saw my dad, what smiles they had on their faces … full of joy. Dad got so happy that he bought me a 3 Musketeer candy bar. You see, this was a big thing in my life. We never had candy. And for Dad to buy me one … What a shock and joy for me! I must have been about 6 years old at the time. Candy never agreed with me though. But, just to think, my dad did buy me some candy. WOW!

That evening, all of us children went to the circus … FREE! But the only thing missing that night was Tom Mix. Tom's double performed for him. You see, Tom and Dad had to sit down and talk old times over again. I was so happy that night because I had never been to a circus or received a candy bar all in one day. Entertainment of such we never had. The only thing I had heard of was our country fair. That was held in Monterey, which was ten miles from where we lived. This was something I never went to.

A great joy for me was to ride on my big swing. It hung from a big limb that grew out of a Eucalyptus tree. Dad really made it nice and I could really swing high. I would swing and sing at the top of my voice. I spent all of my spare time outside, where I enjoyed the beauty of creation. You see, at that time in my life, I didn't know a thing about God. But you see, I knew within me there was someone very special and GREAT. This very special person, I talked to and I thanked Him in person for all the beauty that was around me. I loved the fragrance of the ocean, the lovely fragrance of the sage brush, the lovely stars at night, and the lovely spring flowers. These were special to me and I would always thank this person for all of this.

And this is funny. We had a neighbor named Mr. Brown, and he had a son named Johnny Brown. He spoke with a Scottish brogue, and trained dogs for really wealthy people. They would be hunting dogs. And he made beer in his bathtub! I would see him coming. We lived across the road and railroad tracks from him and his wife. He had this big jacket, which if he was training, he would have a dead rabbit in this side or that side something to help in training these dogs. It was a special jacket that he had. And he would come in and he'd say, "Mary, fill the bucket full of water. Mack and I are having a brew tonight." And he would bring two bottles of his beer. One for Dad and one for him.

His son, Johnny, saved my life one time. We were walking to the beach – my brothers and Johnny Brown. I was so happy that the guys would let me go with them. Oh, boy! Usually, you're a little kid and they don't want you anywhere near. But, I had nice brothers, and Johnny was a nice man. And all of a sudden, I found myself in the air. I would have stepped right on a rattlesnake. And Johnny, he was a tall man, he saw that and he just nabbed me like that, and I didn't get bitten.

MOVING

Now I go back to me as a little girl. My mother, when I was about 2 ½, had to go to the Army hospital in San Francisco. That was a hundred miles away from home. I went to live with my sister, Ruth, and she said she had a terrible time with me because I was always crying for my mother. My mother had to have a blood transfusion. She told me, one day she was lying in bed and a man came up and put his arm next to hers and she received a transfusion from him. My sister, Ruthie, was married by now, so she kept me in her home. I remember Mother stayed some time with me at my sister's home. I don't remember coming home, but I do remember this day as if it were yesterday.

My mother and I left the old ranch house and went into the home that my sister, Ruth, and her husband had built on our property. She didn't like living in this home because she had to travel every day ten miles to go to work. And ten miles at night to come home. Now this was the splitting of my mother and father's life together. I lived with my sister, Gail, my mother, and my brother, Jim. My brother, Sam, had to live with my father. Somehow, I always felt it was because of me coming into this world that their lives broke up. People tell me not to feel this way. The only thing I know, God had His hands on me.

BABY BLUE EYE, BUTTERCUP & POTATO SOUP

Now, I'm older and I'm going to school, and coming home for lunch as always. For we never took lunch to school. Potato soup was our special for lunch. I would enter the kitchen and smell the fragrance. Coming home, as I walked through the grass, I saw two beautiful flowers – one Baby Blue Eye and one yellow Buttercup. I thanked my special person for them because they were so beautiful. But I told this person I would not pick them. They must grow because they're so beautiful. I can still see myself stopping and looking at them and thanking my special friend, as I write about them in this book.

This soup is very simple, so I'm going to add the recipe for you who read this book to enjoy.

Mary's Potato Soup

Potatoes – sliced (not thick)
Onion – chopped (saute if you'd like)
Water
Salt & Pepper

Cook until the potatoes are soft.
With a potato masher – 1, 2, 3, 4 mashes.
Add a good spoon of butter.

ENJOY!

A VISITOR

So, I have to tell you this story. One day while sitting on our back steps and my mother was standing behind me, I spoke to my mother and said, "Mother, how many days would it take Aunt Theresa (my mother's sister) to drive from St. Louis, MO to us here?" We lived in Marina, California.

And my mother looked at me and said, "What in Heaven's name did you get such a thought in your head!" My mother was very angry and said to me, "What goes with you? How did you get such a thing in your head?"

I insisted, "No, Mom. How many days?" Mother made a disgruntled voice and left where she was standing.

Well, that evening, at 5:00, into our driveway came our Aunt Theresa and her daughter, Philomena. When my mother saw them, she told me to GET OUT SOMEWHERE AND NOT TO COME BACK! I never did get to see my Aunt Theresa or her daughter. I only knew my mother had a sister named Theresa. I think my older sisters had told me this. We never ever heard from this Aunt Theresa. Mom never spoke of her again.

Now where did that come from? Somehow my spirit knew she was coming to our home. How different can someone be? I think it must have been things like this that I said at times that would make my mother say to me, "You belong in the old country." I really never understood why she would say this to me.

WORDS OF WISDOM

This day, I was out in the yard. We have quite a yard because we had seven acres of land. And there was a chicken coop, a place for my goat, Nancy, and my swing was there. Oh, my swing – I loved my swing. I saw my father, sitting by his door in his home. And he looked so sad and lonely. Maybe I was about eight years of age, I don't know how old. But I just ran to him as fast as I could. I jumped in his lap, hugged him and I kissed him on the cheek. And my father said, "The last shoe over the fence is the best." Isn't that something?

You know, we weren't brought up in a religion, nothing. But we had good training. My mother always, when we were teenagers, and I left the house, she would say, "Keep your skirts clean." And I knew what that meant.

And my father's big teaching was, "Don't be a herd follower." And that meant, if everybody is doing something stupid – leave. Get away. And I think those two words of advice got me through life. And I think everybody should teach their children. I told my children that.

And last but not least …. Words from my Papa God …. "Beware of those who try to take from you the gifts I have given you.

HEADACHES

Now I must go on as a young girl in grammar school. I loved school and I had a great memory. My only trouble was I had severe headaches. I now have very deep wrinkles on my forehead because I was always trying somehow to move my face hoping that some way I could stop the pain. These headaches stayed with me all the way through grammar school and three years in high school. On my senior year in high school, the pain stopped. My dear, oldest sister, Ruth, had a brain tumor. And when I was in high school, I thought maybe I had one. I went out and had an x-ray taken of my head and the results were intracranial pressure. I called my sister who now lives 100 miles from Mom and I. She told me to come to her and she took me to the medical school that helped her find out that she had a tumor on her 7th nerve in the brain.

I had to take a train to San Francisco and my sister picked me up, and the next day we went to the medical school. I took my x-rays with me and when they read the x-rays, the doctor told me, "What kind of a person read this? They really didn't know how to read them." They gave me a couple tests where they spun me around and then I had to stand on one leg. I passed with flying colors! You see, when my dear sister, Ruth, took this test, she just fell over and they had to catch her. My sister watched me and she was so happy I did not fall. The doctor that tested my sister was a German Jew that escaped from Germany during WWII. He made it here to America. My sister had gone to six doctors before this doctor saw her and they all told her she had war nerves. Thank God for this wonderful Dr. Wartenberg. He saved her life, and his great testing helped show me I did not have a brain tumor. It pays to get the right doctor, don't you think?

WATER

I graduated from high school, but I will tell you this little story. My mom and I had a big water tank and a pump would keep it full. Well, one day, when I was going to catch my bus to school, I walked past one of our garden pipes, and I saw it was leaking. I knew if I didn't fix it, Mother would be out of water. So, I found another piece of pipe, turned the water off, and put a new piece of pipe on. My dad had taught me how to do such things. He knew he was old, and I being the youngest of seven children would probably have to do such things. All went well, but I had missed my school bus. So I had to flag down a Greyhound bus to take me off to school. School was ten miles away. There were so many things I had to do because there was no one to help us.

THE WAR

Now during the start of WWII, I was in grammar school … my last year. My brother, Sam, had just joined the Navy, and on D-Day he came home. I had been to my school watering some geraniums I had planted by our school building. You see, we had a class in agriculture and when we did a special program they gave us a better grade. I love gardening and I was so happy to take care of these plants I was growing for our school to enjoy. I came home from my job and there was my brother, Sam. He told me about the bombing at Pearl Harbor and he had to go to war. I was so upset, that I loved my brother so much to see him die in war. I had two other brothers, and I started to worry that maybe they, too, would also have to go to war. Before this all happened, the many acres that bordered our property were sold to our government and they built a fort on it. It was called Fort Ord. Now with Pearl Harbor happening, our government was afraid California would be the next place they would attack. The Army sent troops over to our land and they dug fox holes under our trees. And at dark, we could not let any lights on in our home. My whole life changed in one terrible day.

I'm quite sure this war was the cause of my father's stroke. It wasn't long after Pearl Harbor that Dad had his stroke. My eldest sister, Ruthie, had to take Dad to the Veterans Hospital, which was at Palo Alto, California. It was seventy-five miles from our home. This now left Mother and myself alone. There was no family close to us. They all lived one hundred or more miles away. My sisters and their husbands all moved to San Francisco, Alameda, and Oakland, California. It was these places that now had jobs. The depression had left our part of California a very poor area to find a decent job.

A couple days after Pearl Harbor, my brother, Sam, brought a wonderful friend home. This friend also went to naval school with Sam, and he was now such a good looking sailor. They were both good looking sailors. I just was looking through some old pictures and there I found this young man's picture. Now the story starts to get sad. Sam and his friend were both assigned to a mine sweeper. Their ship would go in and take out all the mines that were in the water, so the soldiers could land on the shore. When they were under fire, my brother made it behind the bulkhead, but his friend got hit and was blown all over my brother. Sam got blown into the water and had to be rescued. My brother was now in shell shock and had to be placed in a hospital. He was on the island of Guadalcanal, until they could ship him home. War is SO terrible! I just can't see why MAN has to fight all the time.

While Sam was off fighting, my brother, Bob, who was an engineer on ocean ships, now was drafted into the Navy. He went in as an Officer because of his knowledge of ships. My brother, Jim, was a merchant seaman and he worked going up and down the coast of California taking supplies to other ships.

THE SOLDIER

We now had 40,000 troops at Fort Ord, next to our home. One night I woke up hearing my mother saying, "Go home! Go home!" I jumped out of bed, threw on my jeans and a top, went to the living room where Mother was shouting. I had picked up my 22 gun out from under the bed, also. There was a soldier that tore the screen out of our screened in porch door and would not leave when Mother told him to go home. I, being raised by my father, a Teddy Roosevelt soldier, now knew all the terrible words in the English language. I told this man to leave and he told me, "I would like to see you. The girls that speaks with such a terrible tongue."

I told him, "Don't try to come in and see me because he would only see lead."

He knew what I meant. So he hid under a window where we could not see him. I gave my mom the gun, took the safety off, and told her she knew what she had to do if he tried to break in.

I was going to go to my neighbor's home. I knew they had a phone. We had no phone. I had to go through our lower garden, over one big freeway, and over railroad tracks, and then some grass area to get to their home. This was in the dark, maybe at two in the morning. When I got to their home, all their lights were on. They told me this man had come to their home and took a swing at my friend's father. My friend chased him away by getting her gun out. I told them he was on my screened porch. They told me to go up on the highway because they had called the MP's and they were on their way. I did as they said and I flagged the MP's down and showed them where he was. I kind of felt sorry for this soldier because when the MP's got him, they beat him up something terrible.

I learned later from someone that works at the Fort, this fellow did not want to go overseas and probably get killed. So, he thought if he got put in jail, they would not send him. I also learned they would handcuff him, take him on a ship, and once the ship was out at sea, they would release his handcuffs … and he would go to war. That's man and his war.

MY LEO

Graduation was over now and I must get a job. The Fort now was in a way a blessing for our area. People could get more jobs. I went to the unemployment office to see if I could get a job. There was one at a bank and one at the Army dental office. To be a dental assistant, you didn't have to have any experience. They said they would teach me everything I needed to know. I took this job.

The first day I went there, I saw this long two story building. I went into the center door and reported in. They told me to go upstairs and let them know why I was there. I walked up and entered this BIG room with five dental units on each side of the room.

NOW, here is where a new life for me started. As I walked in, in came a dental officer from the other end of the room. He came up the stairs that were on the outside of the building. He smiled at me. I was assigned to a doctor whom I believe was from Puerto Rico, but now was in the Army. The doctor that smiled at me told me much later that when he saw me he said, "Oh my God, there is my wife!"

I worked for this Dr. Aguado until he left and went home. I then went to work for my Dr. Leo. The girl that worked for him was soon to leave because her husband was getting out of the Army. She knew my Leo was sweet on me, and she loved my Leo too much to let him miss working with me. Love was in bloom.

We married in February of 1946. My Leo was sent to Germany soon after. He had it arranged that I would follow him and come to join him in Germany. This I did. I was seven months pregnant with our first child. My Michael was born in Heidelberg. We lived in a town called Feudenheim. This was not far from the city of Mannheim. We went there many times to Mass. The roof of the church was partly blown off. Michael was six months old when we came home.

My Leo was Catholic and I was nothing you might say. I was baptized by a Protestant minister when I was born. I was a premature baby and had to be put in an incubator. My heart had a bad valve. My mother had a VERY bad female condition, and a doctor told her to have another child. Maybe that would help her condition. My poor mother didn't have enough blood for herself, not alone to have a child to take care of in her womb.

Before my Leo and I were married, I became a Catholic. I went to the hospital Army chaplain. And when he talked to me, he said, "You are a Catholic right now." I received my first Jesus on our wedding day.

Now I have to tell you this. I was a different child than the rest of my brothers and sisters. My mother always told me I belonged in the Old Country. And after I was married, my husband even said, "You ARE different! Your mother was right. You are different."

THE CLUB

When my Leo and I returned from Germany, we lived with his mother and father. Leo's dad had a very bad heart condition, and my sweetheart, Leo, knew he would not be with us long. Leo was so happy to spend this time with his dad. Now, as the days went on, I became friends with a very nice lady that lived upstairs in the apartment that was above Leo's parent's delicatessen. She was a young mother with two children. We always visited as we hung diapers on the line. Her name was Genevieve.

Her husband was in a veteran's hospital recovering from tuberculosis. He had been in the air force and was stationed in England. They flew many air strikes over Germany. Gene became like a sister to me.

Now Gene belonged to such a social club. These were all young ladies that were waiting for their husbands or boyfriends to come home from the war. This club was very special to them. And guess what? Due to Gene's mother who loved me, and I loved her, Gene's mother insisted that Gene make sure that I was able to join that club. She knew I had no family here, and all my family was three thousand miles away. She knew I needed this beautiful family of girls. They were all Polish girls and I was the only Irish one in the club. What a great mixture.

Gene's mother, Francis, was such a sweet, happy person, and she made me feel so at home. You had to love her. And even when Halloween came, she came into my mother-in-law's delicatessen store, and she brought a coat and a mask. And she said, "Mary, put this on." Because the party was going to be upstairs in her daughter's apartment. So I put the coat and mask on, and she said, "Go on. They won't know who you are." And she enjoyed that.

So, I did. And it kind of broke the ice, I think, with all of them. The girls, they always dressed up in the funniest things for Halloween. We just had so much fun. I had never in my life met such wonderful, loving, happy women.

There were ten of us in all. We as a group would have meetings every two weeks. At first we would supply a dinner. But then we decided that's too much, so we just would gather and do craft work. But then after we got older, that was out. We had enough crafts.

So what we have been doing now in the last years of our lives, we've been going to lunch together and then to one of our girl's house, who is picked for the meeting. And there we sit and we play "Senior Citizen Rummy." And, oh, everybody is ninety, except me. I'm eighty-seven. And we laugh because we've played this so many years, but still we make some mistakes every now and then. It is a humorous time for us and it's sad to see losing one another. But, we know who the maker is of this beautiful club. It is our Papa God. And every time we meet, we thank Him, especially for giving us this beautiful life.

The husbands died early. All the rest of our husbands died. The last one was my girlfriend, Gene's, husband. And when I would go to him or his wife would talk to him, he always would say, "I sure miss the guys." You see, they moved in with us, in our club. We used to play cards. They came in and they'd go into another room and play penny poker. But, during that penny poker game, they could visit and laugh and joke. We were so gifted by all of these. Can you imagine ten girls at one time getting along for years with no trouble, and then, all our children call us Auntie and Uncle. We weren't related. And to this day, they love our club. My son, Sammy, tells me he can remember when they met at my house. He would be upstairs in his bedroom, and all he heard was laughter and joy coming from us. So, you see, God is good, people. He put ten of us together, who loved Him, and because we loved Him, the club will go down in history. That's a beautiful gift from God.

We now celebrate seventy-four years together. Now there are just four active members. Four have gone to Heaven. One is in Texas, and one in Florida. We miss them, but that is where life takes us and we must go. One girl, (I still call us girls), has a terrible back and spends most of her time in bed. We are now closer than sisters.

POLIO

When I first became a Catholic, I really didn't know Jesus. But Mary… I fell in love with her. I used to go to a Novena to Her on Wednesdays. And I always loved to sing the song, "On This Day, Oh Beautiful Mother". To this day I still love to sing this to Her.

Leo and I had Michael and John, Rosemary, Ann and Sam, but before my John was born, one day after my Leo went to work in his office, I woke up. And when I got up, I just could not swallow. My throat was paralyzed. Even my left side of my face had changed. I called my Leo and he said he would send me to a doctor friend of his who lived not far from his office. And he would have a friend pick me up and take me to this eye, ear, nose and throat specialist. Well, this young man picked me up and when we stopped the car, this gentleman opened the door on his side and a car came and hit it! I went to the doctor, who told me as far as he was concerned I had Polio Myelitis. He called my husband and told him to keep me away from our son. My son was now three years old.

Leo's doctor friend told my Leo he would send me to another doctor downtown and to see what he would say. This doctor said I probably had a cold. When my husband's friend heard this he was furious. He told my sweetheart to put me in bed right away. I was in bed for four days. I did not eat or drink anything. It was Sunday morning, and my Leo made me sit up in bed. My back was stiff. I could not bend over. And my right leg would not straighten out. My Leo told me, when I was in bed he saw my eyes rolling around in my head and I had a big fever. I really didn't remember much of that.

My Leo called an ambulance for me to take me to Millard Fillmore Hospital. You see, there was a big epidemic of Polio at that time, and this hospital had a special wing, just for Polio patients. The men came in from the ambulance with a stretcher, and they laid me on it. They had forgotten the straps to strap me on so I wouldn't fall off. So they left the house to get the straps.

When the two men left, my dear mother-in-law, Rose, came to me. She had in her hands the Polish Sunday paper. It was all in Polish and came out only on Sundays. On the front of this small paper was a picture of Our

Blessed Mother Mary. She told me just to look at Her. I did. And when I did, I felt like someone had lifted a hundred pounds of weight off of me. My Leo came up with tears in his eyes and our little Michael was hanging onto his legs. I could hardly speak because of the paralysis. But the best I could do, I told him not to cry. I was coming back.

They took me to the hospital, and here I almost did myself in. There was water, and I thought I would only take a little too wet my mouth. Big mistake. The water went into my lung and I could not breathe. In panic, how I did this I'll never know. I hung onto the side of the bed somehow, and started to pound my head on the floor. And while I was doing this, a nurse came to the door and asked me if I was dying! I could not speak to her, but my banging my head on the floor did the trick. I now could breathe again.

The intern put a rubber tube down into my stomach so they could give me food and liquids. They did a spinal tap on me right away. One day, a nurse came into my room and while doing needlepoint, watching me to see if I was going to die, she asked me once during this time if she could give me a backrub. I, in panic, told her, "Please! No!" You see, I could hardly stand the sheets touching me. All of my skin was just full of pain.

I made it through three days. I told the intern, "Take this terrible rubber stinking hose out of me." I could not stand the smell and taste. He told me he could not do it because if I could not drink or eat on my own, they would have to put it back in. They shot me full of penicillin. You see, medicine at that time didn't know how to help someone with Polio. They did find out the kind of virus I had, and it was not good. They found this out by the spinal tap. No one could come into the hospital at that time. The epidemic was so bad.

I believe it was the fourth day, I'm really not sure, but Dr. Hyman, came to my door. He had his hands raised up in the air, and he said to me, "Mary, the only one that saved you was the man upstairs."

I, still quite paralyzed, said to him, "I know." You see, my Blessed Mother had stepped in and saved my life.

The hospital moved me to another room and my dear rubber friend was taken out. My sister, Ruth, and my brother, Jim, had come from California. You see, my Leo was sure I was going to die. My Ruthie, then could come to see me. And she brought me a milkshake. You see, when she came the first evening, the first time, she asked me if I had something to eat. And I said no. So, she told the nurse, and they sent me some rice with a soft boiled egg on top. Here I was, on my own, to swallow. I guess the kitchen didn't know that. I did get a little of the milkshake down.

When I could go home, my sister stayed a little longer. My brother went home because he had to take care of my mother. And my dear sister, Ruthie, tried everything she could cook that would be soft, so I could get some food in me. Nothing really made a change in me. Ruthie had to go home. I can remember taking her to the airport. I stayed in the car and my Leo saw her off.

MORE PAIN

Now, that very night, I came down with a big, big pain in my stomach. I pleaded with my sweetheart to call the doctor. He just wouldn't until I got my Irish up and I told him, in no uncertain words, if he didn't do it, I would fall out of the bed and pull the phone down, and call her myself. He knew me, so he finally called the doctor. And she said to bring me right into the hospital. When I walked into the hospital, everyone started yelling, "Get a wheelchair for her!" I looked so terrible. The interns all pushed and checked me out, and sure enough, the surgery was called to take my appendix out. They had to give me a spinal because of my paralysis. I heard the surgeon tell my doctor to move a bowel and be careful. My appendix was very large and it was wound around my intestines. I finally got home from that, but I really looked like an old worn out rag. Now, it took me some time to get my strength back.

FEBRUARY

A couple years later, I gave birth to my son, John. He was 9 lbs. 10 oz. When I went to the hospital to have him, I can remember it was snowing pretty flakes. February was our anniversary and my birthday month. And now, here comes our son, John. He joined us. I had a cough when I went to the hospital, but I didn't think much of it.

When they put me to sleep for a little, and anesthetist had a terrible time waking me up. I could remember him slapping my face and yelling at me, "Wake up!" It just so happened, there was a big flu epidemic. No one could come into the hospital! So, there I sat, all by myself, until they thought I was well enough to go home. See how God was with me?

FAMILY LIFE

My father-in-law had passed away soon after we came from Germany, and my mother-in-law was left with a little delicatessen. This was just too much for her alone. She finally found a home she liked more in the suburbs. She bought it, and Leo and I moved there and had to fix it up. We did fix a little apartment for her, and she could come in and out of our area. And she sold her home and store and all went well. We were all together. We now had Mike, John and Rosemary, with Ann on the way. I became active in my church and I would sing in a little choir … and I do mean little. My Leo, he just became very close to the pastor. And when our pastor died, from a heart condition, my sweetheart was so sad.

When I became pregnant with my son, Sam, I went to the doctor thinking I had an ulcer. But it was not an ulcer, it was my Sammy. Grandma passed away, so me being raised in the country, I asked my sweetheart, "Can we move to the country?" And he said he would look into it. But I knew he wouldn't look into it. I had to look into it. So, I found five different places of country property. And the first place was in North Collins, where I live now. And Leo fell in love with this property. It was just land. We went looking for land everywhere, but Leo would not give up that place. He liked this one, so we bought this property. And we built a home, which we love to this day.

One day, my sister, Ruth, called me and told me she and her husband, their son and his sons friend, their family were going to bring their trailers and come to visit us, because they wanted to see New York. They were all pulling trailers. My Leo was so happy and we knew when they were leaving California. Well, one day we were in our cellar doing something, and my Leo got real angry with me. And he says, "Why haven't you prepared things, so when they come we have steaks and things to BBQ outside?"

I turned to him and said, "They will never get here."

He said, "WHAT! What are you talking about? Why are you saying a thing like that?"

I told him they would have an accident, and I just prayed no one would get hurt. He was so angry with me for what I said. He called me a witch! Well, it wasn't long that day and we got the phone call. It had happened and my sister, Ruthie, got her collar bone broken. Otherwise, they were all okay. They were now turning around and going home. This really upset my poor Leo. Where do these things come to me? He said my dear mother said, "You sure are different." It even worried me.

A SAD DAY

In our new home, we were so happy. We planted trees and had flowers, had chickens, and a vegetable garden. Life was so wonderful. My son, Sam, was going to college, my Mikie had been in the Vietnam War, John served some time in Germany, and their best friend, Archie, was in the Army with Mike. And now John came home and was married. Rosemary had her future husband on the line. Our Ann went off to California to school. Sometimes things were good, and sometimes not so good.

One evening in January 1986, while coming home, my Leo complained of pain in his stomach. I told him, "Let me take you to the hospital to be checked out."

He said no. He would not go. He sat up in our Barcalounger chair. He would not come to bed. I fell asleep, and about three in the morning he came to bed. I was so happy to have him next to me. In a little while, he told me he had to go to the bathroom. And he got up to go and he told me to go back to sleep.

Our Sam, at that time, was still at home living with us. Sam got up before I did and when he went into the kitchen he found his father on the floor. His dad never made it to the bathroom. Sam cleaned his father up before he came to me. Sam woke me up and said to me, "Dad is gone." We both had to carry my sweet one to a couch. Now my life was gone for sure.

HICCUPS

Soon after all of this, I was called to go to Monterey. My brother, Jim, had broken his hip and they needed me, next of kin, to be there with him. My son, Michael, called me early in the morning to tell me they needed me. I told him I would call him back after I came from church. While driving from church a song came into my head. The words were, "Go forth among the people. Tell men of every nation. Tell them Christ has died for sin, so a new life could begin. Let them know he came to bring salvation."

I came home and I called Michael and I told him I would go Thursday, but not Wednesday, because I had to go to my prayer meeting in Hamburg. But, you know, singing that song and it says salvation, I knew I had to go. While at the meeting I raised my hands to the Lord. "What about my brother, Jim?" I said to my God. God said, "He'll be fine."

So, off I went to my old home town. Jim was on life support when I got there, so I could only stay with him for a short time. When I left him, I would go to his trailer he had, and I would clean it up. Because, being an alcoholic, Jim kept a little in need of cleaning. I used his little Toyota for my transportation. He had a bolt missing out of his alternator, so I had to get that fixed, so I could drive the car. This was why Jimmy broke his hip. It wouldn't start. So, with one leg out of the car, he would push and try to start the car that way … by rolling it along and then releasing the clutch.

Jim was heavy on drinking and this was a BIG problem. The doctor that took care of Jim had lost a patient that jumped out of a window in a hospital, because of being an alcoholic. So Jim, they gave him an overdose, so he wouldn't be jumping around. They found Jimmy not breathing. And they had to resuscitate him and bring him back to life. They brought him back to life and then they found out that he had internal bleeding. They gave him a colostomy. When I saw Jimmy, he was just about alive. I sat next to him as much as I could and I would pray over him.

One night when I was going home, I happened to walk right into a man's room. I saw him many times walking around and talking to people, and he would have visitors. This man looked so strong and healthy. I asked him, "Why are you in this hospital?"

He said, "I've had hiccups for three months. And they were trying to find out what was causing them." He asked me if I had a remedy. I told him I would hold his ears shut and he would drink water. He right away jumped up on his bed with his glass of water and we tried it.

Nothing happened he said. But you see, he saw my crucifix on my chain around my neck and in a real nasty voice, he said, "You are a Christian, aren't you!"

I said, "Yes I am a Christian."

And in a very nasty voice he said, "My God would never come down in the form of a man!"

I told him, "That's your belief. Jesus is my salvation. And God bless you and good night."

I wondered why I went into this man's room because he was so nasty to me and to Jesus.

Two days later, my brother-in-law and I were waiting to go to see Jim. They were cleaning his bed and getting him ready for the night. I, just being born again, I talked about our Jesus all the time. And whoever was near me heard about Jesus. And Herman, I don't think appreciated that. Herman got up and said he was going to go see if Jim was ready.

He left and in a few minutes I got up and went right straight into that man's room. I asked him how he was. And he said they were going to open his skull. I said to him, "Boy that is serious!"

With that, he jumped up, got his glass of water, and said, "Let's try your remedy again."

This time, I closed my eyes, held his ears shut, and I guess he was drinking the water. And in a little bit, I heard him. He was saying some words I didn't understand at all. And you see, I didn't see him at all while this was going on. After a couple minutes, he yelled, "They are gone! They are gone!" He screamed! He scared me half to death. He flailed his arms in the air. What an experience for me. He jumped up on his pillow and said, "Let's talk about your Jesus."

A voice came to me like from the back of my head and out of my mouth and it said, "You must rest. You must rest." And I left his room. The next day he was not there, and I never saw him again.

This was a start for me in a new life. Jim came home with me, and I planned to stay for a while with him, but God had other plans.

NOW I GO TO MY PEOPLE

When I came home from my first trip to California to help my brother, who was very, very ill, the people in our church asked me if I would like to be a Eucharistic Minister. They said they were going to have a group teaching for this, and whoever wished to participate in this would be allowed to take it. My first being born again, I, of course, was really excited, and I said, "Yes, I'll take this course."

Now, this is so beautiful. The very first day I was on duty at our church, to serve my God, as I walked up to the altar, a voice (very strong) said to me, "Now, I go to my people." I was so surprised. I was lucky I made it to the altar. Now, every time I go to Communion, I always watch the people receiving Jesus, and these words, "Now, I go to my people" comes out of me. If ever I had doubt about the Eucharist being Jesus, that doubt is gone forever. God showed me with such a beautiful way how He is in that host.

Can you really love a God like our God? He is here for each and every one of us. I always tell Papa God to keep me under His mantle. I always tell Jesus, Holy Spirit, and our Blessed Mother to keep me under their mantles, too. We need to be close to our Master Jesus. He came to help teach in how we should love one another, as He loves us. It is so beautiful. Don't you think? I pray you will always love your Heavenly Family. I talk to them all the time. This life is so beautiful when we know and love our Heavenly Family.

PRAYER FRIEND

Now, one more story. This happened I 1989. The Charismatic group I knew invited us to go to Christ the King Seminary for a day of prayer. We were to brown bag it. With this all being so new to me, I was happy to go. I believe there must have been 40-50 of us there. The leader told us to form a circle and we were to put our hands on the person in front of us and pray for that person. Then to turn around and do the same to the other person who had been in back of us. This I did, but for some reason, out of all of us, I went out in the Spirit and as I was lying on the floor, I was sobbing. Why me? I didn't know. But, finally, this nice gentleman came and picked me up and sat me on a chair and held my hands. This was a starting of a longtime friendship.

You see, the young man who has offered to help me with my book is the son of this man. They have really been family to me. So close are we that when I went to put a large cross up on my property, my prayer friend came to my home and helped put the cross up.

ROBERT

My Rosemary married and had her second boy. Robert was born with
Spina Bifida. He is so sweet, our Robert. People just love him so much.
He is special. Rosemary had worked with my husband in his dental office,
but when Robert came, she had to give up work. I then went to work for
my sweetheart. It was nice to be with him all the time.

There was trouble at home and I had to go home. My dear brother-in-law,
Herman, said he would take care and watch over Jimmy. When I got home,
my daughter, Rosemary, and her three children, moved in with me. We
were very happy together. Her eldest child, Johnny, made his First Holy
Communion in our church. Robert was the little guy with the Spina Bifida.
He would never walk … ever.

It was next year after Johnny was given Communion that the women in our
church decided that Robert should make Communion. They knew his
problem was a serious one … Spina Bifida and all paralyzed from the waist
down. He went with a group of children to begin classes and I remained in
the church. It was not long, and in came our pastor speaking out loud.
"He is too young. He cannot make Holy Communion."

When I heard this from his lips, I thought my heart would break. You see,
Robert was raised by so many wonderful, older people, that he was more
advanced than the other children. Now I must tell you, I held this against
our pastor.

It was Christmas, and we were having four extra priests to help with our
Confession. I knew I had to go to Confession. You see, the Lord told me,
if I did not confess this sin against our pastor, I would not grow in the
Lord. When the evening came, I went to church really wondering how I
could do this. Well, I went half way down the church and sat in a pew.
And when I saw that there were just a few people in line for our pastor, I
got up and I started down the aisle. As I did this I heard angels shouting,
"She's gonna do it, she's gonna do it, she's gonna do it!" They were helping
me.

I had help cheering me on. When I confessed my sin of holding against my
priest for not letting Robert receive his Communion, my pastor said to me,

"You either have a lot of faith or a lot of guts." I cried like a baby as I left my pastor.

My Rosemary and I enjoyed her stay with me. One day, my Robert came home from school and the bus driver brought him up to the door. Robert was in a wheelchair. As Robert came wheeling up to me, he said, "Grandma, were you sad today?" I told him, "Yes, Robert," because it was the truth and he could see it in my face. He came up to me, jumped in my lap, and told me he had felt bad today. And as he was going back to class from having the nurse catherize him, he then told me how he shouted out, "This is not the way to act!" He told me this just so powerfully, I had to grab him and kiss him. Here he was, so terribly worse off than I ever was. And he was teaching me how to live my life.

Then, later one day, Robert told me he was worried about a kidney test he had to have. I told him, don't worry because I knew of a priest from Canada, who is having a Healing Mass at the Shrine of Fatima in Lewiston, and we would go there and he would be prayed over and God would help him. Well, this we did. Robert, I and his little sister, Nicole - we went to the Mass, and then when it was time, Robert wheeled himself up to the priest and told the priest what his problem was. Nicole and I stayed aside. And there were many people praying behind this priest. As the priest touched Robert's head with his hands, Robert went out in the Spirit. His head just fell back. We all stood around praying, and kept praying for Robert. When Robert came too, tears were just pouring down his cheeks. The priest asked him, "Robert, why are you crying?" He said, "I don't know."

I do now know, as I did then, Robert received the Holy Spirit. When Robert went to high school, if there was a child that needed counseling, they would all go to Robert for strength.

He was given a special gift from God. Today, the same goes on with him. He is 31 years of age and a cashier at Wegmans in Amherst. People come to him special - to be in his line. Many people tell him they wish he could talk to their child. Some hockey players would bring him donuts and things to eat.

You see, man denied him, but God did not. I wish everyone who reads this book could talk to Robert. He truly is a gift from God. He says to me, the way he is today is because of three women in his life – his mother, his grandmother, and his sister.

What a beautiful, blessed child God gave us. Robert is a beautiful, blessed person and always will be. You see what God showed us? God is in control.

SAINT PADRE PIO

Now do you see what our God can do? As Saint Padre Pio says, "Pray, hope and don't worry." If you need someone to help you, take Padre Pio as a close friend and pray to him. He really will help you.

Let me tell you this story. This is a story to really make you think. It has to do with this special saint. I had read the story of his life maybe seven years ago, and for some reason I felt a need to read about him again. My dear friend, Cathy, when I told her how I wanted to read about him again, told me her daughter had recently purchased Padre's latest new addition, and she was sure she would let me read it. This I did and became so close to him as a special person in my life. This is someone I can talk to in certain instances.

Well now, wait till you hear this …

Whenever I leave my car before going into Mass, I lock it. This one day, after Mass, as I opened the door, out came such cigarette smoke. It was like maybe twelve people had been smoking in it. I opened all the windows and drove kind of fast hoping to get this terrible smell out of my car. I told my daughter and my daughter-in-law about this. They couldn't figure out why this had happened. I even told my priest about this.

Well, in a couple weeks, my Rosemary calls me on the phone, screaming at me about me and Padre Pio. She said to me, "What's up with the cigarette smoke?"

You see, she was driving in her car when all of a sudden her car was just full of cigarette smoke. She said she felt like vomiting, it was so bad.

Now, about four weeks later, my daughter-in-law, Grace, and her husband, my son John, came out to visit with me. When Grace and I were alone, she came to me and almost whispered to me. "Mom, your son has had that same experience you and Rosemary had with the cigarette smoke."

What do you think my friend was trying to tell the three of us? I'm sure someday we'll find out, but I just know he was letting us know his spirit is here for us. I know many people other than Catholics cannot understand how we pray to saints.

What do you think about this? I even told my priest about this. I see us as a people who do not know a thing about the spiritual life that is around us. We must pray to our Heavenly Father and ask him to teach us and show us more about this life we have here on this earth. We do not understand the spiritual world at all.

THE APPLE ORCHARD

So I must tell you, when my sweetheart first died and I was home, I needed money. Because at my dental office was not being used, there was no money coming in there. Money was short. My church needed somebody to clean the church and the rectory. And I would get $70 a week. That sounded good to me. At least I would get gas for the car.

So, I would always go into church early and say my Stations of the Cross. This day happened to be a Saturday morning. We still had the nuns. And we never had church Saturday mornings in the church. It was always in the convent. The nuns had a little chapel there. And this Saturday, I walked into the church and the light was on behind Jesus and the crucifix. And I said, "Boy, Father must be having somebody coming later to church, because there is no Mass in here. So now, I went up and knelt at my first station. The door opened about three inches and the voice of our pastor, said to me, "Did you leave the front door open?"

I said, "Yes, it's unlocked."

As I knelt there to say my first station, I looked up at Jesus on the cross. And what I saw – I almost fainted. His chest was moving in and out, and the muscles in his arms were moving.

I got to the second station. I'm saying, "God, what is wrong with me? Am I going crazy? Why am I seeing such a thing? Please, help me!" And I'm crying.

When I got to the third station, I was sobbing so hard looking at Jesus. I ran to the altar, knelt down and looking up at Jesus, I said, "Please, don't cry. I love you." And with that, everything stopped and the last thing I saw was the left arm muscle stopped moving.

Well, I went to the other stations, but by the time I got to the seventh station, I was crying again. By the time I got to the tenth station, I thought, "Oh, dear God, it's late. The priest is going to be coming through and he's going to be wondering what I'm doing here. So, I ran out. I had to go outside to go to the chapel. And while I'm outside, I'm thinking in my head, "Oh, my God. I'm gonna have a big red nose from crying. What are people gonna say when they see me?"

So, I went into the chapel and I sat in the very last pew. And when I went up to Communion, I held my head kind of down. Then I came back and I said, "Who can I tell this to?" We had the two nuns, Sister Marietta and Sister Julia. I felt I could tell Sister Julia, because she had charge of Villa Maria at one time.

While I'm kneeling there with my head down, not seeing anybody, I soon heard footsteps coming, and it was Sister Marietta. And she said to me, "What do you think you're gonna do? Sit in here all day?" And with that, I jumped up and ran out. And as I went out of the building, I started crying again.

Well, then I went to get the paper for my brother, and as I started driving up the hill to my home, there was a young man carrying a big Styrofoam lunch basket and a Styrofoam thermos type container. It was a real misty day. Oh, it wasn't raining, but it was so misty. And, I pulled my car over. Something I would never do. I said, "Get in this car. You're gonna be dripping wet, where ever you're going." So, he got in. And I said, "Where are you going?"

"I'm going to pick apples."

I said, "Apples! There's no apple orchards up here in this area."

"Oh, yes there are. I picked apples here yesterday."

I said, "Well, I'll take you." So I drove clear up to Langford. Now I'm getting kinda scared. Who is this I have in my car? There is a little delicatessen there and I said, "I'll stop here and you go over there and talk to the people in that store. And I'll turn the car around in case we have to go further up, because I'd never been further up there at any time. He came out and he said, "No, there's no apple orchard here, but I know I was here yesterday."

I said, "Well, we'll go up a little further and as I started to go there was a man washing a boat. And I said, "Sir, is there an apple orchard here somewhere?"

"No! It's on Shirley Road." And I knew where Shirley Road was.

So I said, "Fine!"

And we turned around and he said, "No! That's not the place."

Well, as we drove to Shirley Road, I told him about my episode in church with Jesus. And he said to me, "Too bad you can't talk to the leader of our prayer group here.

And I told him, "I never heard of a prayer group here in North Collins."

He said, "She could really help me with this experience I had in church."

I'm thinking, North Collins. There's no prayer group here. There's only one in Hamburg. So, when we got almost to this apple orchard on Shirley Road, I knew where he had to go. We were going east and we had to go west. So, I said, "I'll get you there. I know where you're going. (Because when my brother-in-law had come to visit me after my sister died, I took him to this place, and we picked apples. My brother-in-law was so happy. He told me never in his life did he ever pick apples.) " Since, I've been here, Mary, I'm having so much fun." He would pick corn. I had corn growing in my garden. And he loved it so much.

So, anyway, I got this young man to where he was to go pick apples. He said to me, "This is it!"

I said, "Wonderful."

As he got out of the car and started walking away, I just got the strongest feeling that Jesus was walking away. I started praying in tongues. You won't believe how I was praying. I said, "Lord, you really did me in this Saturday! I'm exhausted!"

THE ARROW

And now, here is one more that I really don't understand at all. I think it happened around 1989 or 1990. I received this job at our church, for they needed someone to clean up the church. And I was hurting for money, so I took the job. As I said before, I always went to church early, so I could pray the Stations of the Cross. My dear friend, Anna, would come in later, and we always sat in the third pew, on the left side of the church, where our Blessed Mother is.

I had finished my Stations, and as I walked up the outside aisle, my friend came in and she was sitting next to my purse. And she spoke up to me. "What are we doing back here?"

I said, "I don't know." You see I had left my purse in a pew half way down the church.

As I turned to enter into the pew, as God is my witness, the priest just took one or two steps out into the altar area, from the sacristy, and I felt like I got struck by an arrow, right in my chest. Wow! I said, "Lord, what is going on here?" It really was terrible.

But, being the tough old gal I am, I went in and sat down by my friend. And that's where we spent our Mass time – halfway back in church. What this all meant, I have no idea. But, it sure wasn't a very lovely experience.

JIMMY STAYS WITH ME

Now for more news. I had to go back to California again because my brother had gone back to drinking and they found him lying on the floor. He was now a diabetic and he was in a diabetic coma. When they found him, they took him to the hospital and of course, they found out he really is a diabetic now. And he could not take care of himself because he had lost a finger due to stenosis from smoking, and could not give himself a shot of insulin. When he was better and at home, I told him, "Jimmy, you either go to a nursing home here or you come home with me."

And he said, "I will come home with you, if you take my dog."

He had this big dog called Sara Doo. He named her Sara Doo because when he brought her home, the first thing she did was doo-doo in the house. That was my brother, Jim's, sense of humor.

At this stage now, Jimmy was with me and it was a very lovely time for me, because he was my special brother. I loved him so much, because when I was a little girl, he watched me. If I was sick, he would come specially into the bedroom and ask me what I wanted. And he would go to the store and get whatever I wanted. And then when he got sick, I always knew what he wanted. He wanted oyster stew. I would go to the store and get the can of oysters and mother would make him oyster stew. When he would be working on his car, I was always by his side to run get the tools he would need.

When I would go home with my children in the summertime to visit my mother and the family, my Jim did many things for me and my children. He made a special tent for us to sleep in. The children and I loved to sleep outside in a tent. Also, he fixed a lovely place where I could have breakfast with my children and have our meals. And he made toys for my kids. And he took us fishing. And my Johnny learned how to drive a Jeep. The biggest joy in Jimmy's life was when his Muggsie was coming home for the summer.

He was a wonderful brother. It was nothing for me to take care of him. We were so close together, that to me to have Jimmy was really a blessing for me, because he loved me and I loved him.

I would wake up at 5:30 in the morning and bathe him, clean his bed up, feed him his breakfast, and then I was on my way to church. I would raise the sides of his bed up so he couldn't get out of bed. Poor guy. He was stuck, but I knew he was safe.

I knew my Jimmy, when he was young, he liked to read his daily newspaper. So, I always stopped after church and got the newspaper for him. I knew he couldn't register much in his brain anymore because the alcohol had done such damage to him, but I wanted him to have his newspaper that meant so much to him.

THE CASHIER

Now this one day, after church, I went to pick up Jim's newspaper, and there was a lovely lady as a cashier at our old store down here. And she always looked so down. One day, she said to me, "Where do you go to church?"

I said, "To the Holy Spirit Church."

"You don't go there," she said. "You're not like those people."

I said, "Sorry, Honey. That's where Jesus is and that's where I go."

So one day, I said to her, "Honey, you look so sad. What is the trouble?"

And she said, "I'm going through a terrible divorce."

So, I looked at her and said, "Go to your boss and tell him you want five minutes off and we'll go outside, and I'll pray over you."

So, she did as I asked her to do. And, after the prayer, she went back to work and I went home. And you know what she told me when I saw her the next time? She said, "That prayer changed my whole life."

When I saw her next I told her, "Honey, don't hate your husband. Pray for him, and it'll help you. Because when you pray for somebody like this, you're the one who will receive help from God.

So she told me later on, "Mary- that was the best thing you could have told me. Now I'm at peace. I have no anger towards him." This was the Holy Spirit's work.

THE CROSS

Now, I'll tell another story. I had brought my brother here because there was no place for him in California. He did not want to go to a nursing home. So, as the story I've told, I would always get up and get everything ready for him, and then go to church. Well, this day, as I started to drive out of the driveway, on the first turn, I looked up. And there in the sky was this HUGE, big cross. And it was not standing straight up. It was at the position like Jesus was still carrying it. It was kind of brownish and it looked like it had blood on it. I said, "Lord, what is this?" And I went on to church.

The next day, I go again to church. Now this really amazed me, because I never see things twice, as a rule. But, as I go on that turn, here is this HUGE cross – again! The same one, in the same position. I said, "Whoa! Papa God, what are you showing me?"

Now, the third day, I had the same experience. There, as I drove on the turn, was this HUGE cross in the sky. The same one. And I said, "Wow! Three times in a row, Papa God. What is going on?" So, I kept thinking about this. And then I thought, well, maybe I should put a cross on my property here. And let it face in that direction, where I saw the cross in the sky.

I have a dear friend at church, who is a guitar player and he is in our music ministry. I bought the wood I needed for the cross, and he built this nice cross for me. Friends helped me put it up on my property. We faced it in the direction where I saw these crosses in the sky. From the road, you could see it. Well, guess what? One day, there was a can of Campbell's pork and beans put in my mailbox. I had to clean that up. It seems like people in the area didn't like the cross.

The next time, there is no mailbox. I went to the police station, to ask them if we could do something about this. Well, as I walked in, there was my orange mailbox up on the counter. Someone had taken it and threw it on a different road. And the policemen knew by the color that it was mine. So I retrieved it, and now I put a black mailbox up. And so far, no trouble.

I had to remove my cross, because the gas company drilled for gas on my property. And it had to be right where my cross was! So, the cross was taken down. And for some time, because I couldn't put it up, it was laying near my driveway.

But then one day, my youngest son, Sam, said, "Mom, I'm gonna put the cross back up."

I said, "Well, Honey, you'll have to have help, because that's not a tiny cross."

You know, he did it by himself. And I said to him, "Sam, how did you do that?"

"Well," he said, "Mom, I guess I had a lot of angels around helping me, because it was really a hard job!"

So, now as I'm writing about this, yesterday, my son came and he cut the grass all around my cross. And he made a pathway, so we can go there. I used to have big rocks to sit on and rest. When they put the gas well in, they threw them in a big hole. So, now I have to put a little bench out there, so I can sit and pray by my cross.

THE SONG

Now, the song… One day, just like any other day, all of a sudden, out of my mouth came this strong, spiritual song. I didn't understand it at all. It was something new to me. This song, then, would come out sometimes when I would go into church. My friends would say, "Mary is here!" Sometimes when I would be leaving the church, it would come out again. It made me so happy when the Spirit would do this. I can do it, if I wish to do it, but I prefer to allow the Spirit to be in control.

One day, while leaving the church after mass, this song came out. It was really beautiful. And as the song came out, a priest passed by me and made an ill remark about it. After this happened, the song would not come out. It was such a long time until it came out again.

One day, as I entered the hallway leading to our church, our little chapel, a very small song came out … and very little. I spoke to it and said, "You're still here? I missed you." I truly felt if someone denies the Spirit, He will leave. This is sad. I know this is hard for you to believe, but it is true. The name of our church is Holy Spirit Church. I miss my dear friend. I pray someday He will return in full song again. And that's the truth.

POTTING SOIL

Now, listen to this little story of God working. Remember, I'm just a little worker that gave her life to God. You see, God needs people that will do what he wants them to do. And I'm willing, always, to do whatever God wished me to do.

Now this story started about 2006. My son, Sam, and his wife and family had an opportunity to go spend some time in Florida at a condo that was owned by his friend. My daughter, Rosemary, had charge of watching over his delivery service. And I had charge of making sure all coming in finances were put in the bank, right away. This day, Rosemary had to pick up a large box of tee shirts that had been printed on and they had to be delivered to another place, quite a distance away. I said I would go with her, but first, we had to go to the bank. She agreed. So, off we went to the bank.

Half way coming back from the bank, I told my Rosemary, "I need to buy some potting soil. Some of my plants had to be repotted."

She said, "Ok, Mom. Let's get it right now, because we are not far from the garden center."

We drove in, and as a rule, I would park up on a little hill. But this day, the big doors were open on the side of the building. And I knew what I needed was right there. I parked alongside the building, and we could just walk right in. I showed my daughter what it was that I needed, and I was going to go in and pay the gentleman in the other room.

You see, there was a door I had to go through to get into this other room. There was this elderly gentleman there cashing out another customer. I opened the door, and there happened to be this man just finishing paying this elderly gentleman. The man saw me and he said to the elderly man, "I hope you feel better. I must leave because you have another customer." (Meaning me) The elderly gentleman was so pale. He was grey and looked so sick.

Now I wish you could have heard this. I walked up to the elderly gentleman, and I said in a terribly strong, loud voice, "Are you sick?"

He answered me. He said he had pneumonia, and just could not seem to get strong and well again after it.

Out of my mouth came these words. "Do you know Jesus?"

He didn't say a word. He just lowered his head down near the counter. In the same gruff, strong voice I said, "I know Jesus, and keep your head down there. I'm going to pray over you."

I first said my little short prayer that I always say before I pray over anyone. It's a protecting prayer for me. And then I put my hands on his head, and his head was warm. How I prayed, I can't tell you. Whether it was in tongues or English, because this was the Holy Spirit's work – not mine. Never in my life would I speak to somebody the way I spoke to this poor, little old gentleman.

Believe me, when the prayer was over, I told him what I had picked out and I wanted to pay him. And this I did. I paid him and left the room, and went back to the room where I had told Rosemary to put these items in the car, because that's what I needed. And you know me, an old lady, I had to check to make sure it was in the car. I went to get into my car, though, because I was the driver. Rosemary was not insight anywhere. She was out looking to see just what they had to offer.

Well, I reached for the car door, to open it up. And when I looked up, there was the elderly gentleman, standing in the open room. His cheeks were full of beautiful color. He looked in perfect health. I was so shocked to see him like this. What a transformation! Now, there was one terrible, frightening thing. The man's eyes did not look like eyes. They were bright lights. Something like some of the new cars have. They frightened me because they were so bright.

My daughter came up and we got into our car, and went off on our pickup business. All I can say is, I felt different all day long. This is one experience of a lifetime.

Now about two years later, as I walked into my Hamburg prayer group, there was a young lady, who I had never seen before. But she knew me by name. Maybe twenty-five minutes later, in came her husband, and he was quite upset. I won't go into that, though. But, later on in the evening, for some reason, I told them the story that had taken place with this elderly gentleman. And the young man said to me, "I know that man. He lives on my street. He has children. And the children always went to church, but he never went to church. Now, he was in church with his family, all the time."

Some people ask me if I ever went to talk to him about what had happened. I told them no. Because that was not my part. That was the Holy Spirit's doing. I was just a vessel that God needed, and His Holy Spirit knew He could use me. That's the truth.

About those eyes. A few months after this had happened, I told a lady at one of our church meetings about it. And she said she knew why his eyes were bright like that. Boy, she was pretty smart, I thought. And she said that was the Light of Christ, coming through him. What do you think?

HEALING

Now I always go to my Wednesday night prayer groups, and if there's a special Charismatic meeting, I always wanted to go there. One evening, I went to one and it was quite some time ago. And after the program I was just sitting on a removable stage, and a lady, who I didn't know at all, came up to talk to me. And as she sat down, I saw she had trouble with her knee. While talking to her, I just rubbed her knee. I didn't think of praying over her or anything. And after a while, we got up and she went her way and I went mine. I don't even know this lady.

Now it must have been three years later, I was at another meeting. And this lady came running up to me saying, "You're the lady that healed me!"

I told her, "Honey, I don't heal anyone. God is the healer."

And she said, "Well, it was you that rubbed my knee that night, and it was healed."

I told her to be happy for the healing and make sure she gets down and thanks Papa God for the healing. You see how God works? He only needs a heart that loves Him, and someone who will be obedient to Him. I tell Him all the time that I love Him and to use me for His glory.

RALPH

Now here's another story. The priest we had at this time, had a severe pain in his shoulder. And as I heard from others, he had gone everywhere, trying to get help. Even for some of our parishioners, they thought maybe they could pray and it would get better. Well, I knew this problem. So, one day, early, as I'm always in church early, Father was there. And I said, "Father, how's your shoulder?"

Oh, he got disgruntled. He said, "I've tried everything, and nothing works."

And I said, "Well, Father God – sometimes He heals people if I lay hands on them and pray." I said, "Would you like to give it a shot?" I spoke like he does because he always spoke kind of rough.

"Ok," he said. So, we went into the sacristy and Father sat down. I don't know how I prayed over him. Whether it was in tongue, whether it was in English, I don't even remember. But I did pray. And all of a sudden, Father said, "That's enough!" And he got up and went out.

I said, "Fine."

So, I usually sat on my Blessed Mother's side of the church. For some reason, this day I went and sat on the side of Joseph. The right hand side of the church. And Mass started. Many times I have a habit of looking down, not looking up. And as I lifted my head up and saw Father at the altar, I couldn't believe what I saw. There on Father's left side was a HUGE wing. From the top of his shoulder, to the floor. I'd never ever seen anything like this. It had to be, the way the wing was, they tell me Guardian Angels have these long, tall wings.

Well, I was really shocked. But I knew I couldn't tell Father this Sunday, because he was in a hurry always to go to the prison and have Mass for the prisoners. So, I had to wait a couple days. And it just so happened, on the second day, I go in and there's Father. And I said, "Father, how are you feeling?"

He answered, "I hate to admit it, but I feel better!"

So, then I said, "Father, I have to tell you this. You remember how I prayed over you?"

"Yeah!"

I said, "Well, at the altar when you were standing there, I saw this HUGE wing, from your left shoulder all the way down to the floor."

And he looked real, like frightened … scared. I said, "Father, don't be frightened or scared. God sends angels with healing for us."

And with that, he said, "Yeah, it was probably my Guardian Angel, Ralph."

SUN – SON

Well, here's another story. I'm always talking to Papa God because He is my strength. And I know He has guided me through my life. I have my dear friend in church. This nice guy that made my cross for me. And he plays the guitar for our music ministry. One day he asked me if I would go to Our Lady of Perpetual Help Church, where he was going to be in the music ministry. It was an eight day Mission. He told me, "You're always good at singing and you could get the people really into the feeling of the Mission." And he knew how I loved to sing, so he asked me. And I thought, well, maybe I can help with the music ministry. I told him I would love to help out.

Well, that special Sunday did come. And I got into my car and going down my driveway, I looked up and I saw in the sky, over where this church was, off of Route 20, rain clouds. So, guess what I did? I right away started talking to Papa God. "Father, please, see to it that it doesn't rain this evening. Because, if it does, people will not come to the Mission. And they will not learn more about you, and they will not learn more about your mother." This conversation just kept going all the way through the woods, before I could reach the main highway.

I had to turn off of the highway at Route 62, to the road that would lead me to where the next road would take me to the church. As I drove, I looked up as I crossed some train tracks. And there was a great big opening between some trees. And there was the sun. I said, "Papa God, thank you. You did hear me. And now the people will come." And I actually slowed down, almost to a stop, because I was so happy to see this beautiful sun shining there.

Well, guess what happened now? I almost fainted. There was as if you took a magic marker four inches wide. And a big, red heart was placed around the sun. I was so amazed at what I saw. I said, "Wow! What is this?" And yet, as I drove on now, I said, "I can't tell anybody this. They won't believe me." But listen to this, people. When I got to that Mission, and I was leading the music, I'm telling you – I was on fire! And those tongues really flew out of me. And Ted was happy, my guitar player. Because the people got right into the swing of it and they were singing.

You see what God does? He shows us things.

But then, later on, I kept thinking about this heart around the sun. And one day, as I was driving to the Indian Reservation to get gas, I was talking to my Papa God. I said, "Papa, what was that with that heart around the sun?" And this is what came to me. "Without the sun, you would have no life on earth." Wow! What a revelation that was. How true. Without that sun, and yes, that sun is in His heart. That's how much He loves us, people. So remember to thank Father God, every time you see that sun.

Well, this isn't the end of the story. One day, while going to work, I'm talking to my Papa God. And I'm talking about that heart around the sun. I'm telling him it was beautiful. But, it really was hard for me to understand the whole thing. And He said to me, "I have two sons. One s-u-n and one s-o-n. One gives you life on the earth, and one gives you eternal life." I got to work that day. I think I drove my poor son crazy. Because I was so full of the Spirit, so happy! And I said, "Oh, see what a God we have! Look what He gives us and people don't want to know him. What He has planned for us. All these beautiful trees, all these beautiful breaths that we take, every day. You sleep. You wake up. You eat. All gifts from God.

ALEX

Now, as I was so excited with the Lord, I don't even remember how I found this out. But, there was a bus load of people going to go to Notre Dame, because they were having a seminar and the main speaker was this priest, who has so much to do with the children in Medjugorje. And, boy, I had read the story of Medjugorje, so I wanted to go. And I did. When we got to Notre Dame, I spoke to the lady who was in charge of the bus. I said, "I don't know anything about Notre Dame here. I don't know where I will stay, where we eat, or anything."

And she said, "Don't worry. I have two ladies right here and they've been to Notre Dame before. And they will help you. I'm sure your lodgings are in the same building, and so they'll watch over you. Don't worry."

So, they did. They showed me everything around there. Where to go to eat. And I was very content. I couldn't wait for the last day, because it was on the last day when this priest would come and give us the beautiful talk.

Well, the day arrived. One of the ladies had diabetes very badly, and she was rather heavy set. The two ladies liked to sleep in later than I. And, so, the day we were to leave, I knew we were supposed to have all of our luggage out in the parking lot at six in the morning, so it would be picked up and put on our bus. Well, I had one little tote bag. That's all I had. I could carry it. But they had large quantities of blankets and everything. So, when I got together with them, I said, "Girls, I don't think we're gonna find the bus. I think it's gone already."

And they said, "Well, come on. We'll go out there anyway." And they were pulling all this heavy luggage. I felt so sorry for the girl that was heavy and diabetic. So, we went out by the road across from the parking lot. And there was a bench there. So, we sat down. And as we started to talk, I asked them if they knew the name of their guardian angel, because I named mine. And I named him Alex. Because this beautiful picture I have of my Blessed Mother of Perpetual Help and my first bible were given to my husband and I, because my husband always did all the work for priests and nuns for nothing, (he never charged them for the work he would do). Father Alexander, who had charge of the choir singing at St. Francis School, was his patient. And one night, in a dream, I saw this man. And I knew it was Father Alex. I said that's my Father Alexander, and that's my guardian angel.

So, I told them my story. And the girl that was the diabetic, she said her guardian angel's name was Joel Ann. I said, "Joel Ann. That's a strange name." To me it was a strange name because I had never heard it before. And the other girl had never named her guardian angel.

So, as time was going on, it was getting late. And I knew the bus wasn't going to come. So, all of a sudden, the Spirit hit me. I jumped off from sitting on the bench, and I went out to the edge of the road. Raising my hands up in the sky, I yelled, "Papa God, we need an angel!"

And if you want to believe this or not, instantly, a white car drove up, and a woman pops out. She asks, "Are you in trouble?"

And I told her the problem. I said, "These girls can never walk that distance with all their luggage. And I said, "We really need some help to get to the auditorium."

"Don't worry." She opens her trunk. "Come on. We'll put all of your stuff in my trunk." And she said, "At 1:00, I'll be at the parking lot by the auditorium. And you come out, and you can pick up your luggage, put it in the auditorium by the doorway, and when the bus comes, they'll just put it on the bus."

Well, all I had was just this one tiny tote bag. So, it really didn't bother me at all. She took us all in her car and dropped us off. On the way to the auditorium, I asked this lovely lady what her name was. She told us Joel Ann. Whew, talk about God and His surprises!

Well, these two ladies decided they were gonna go look somewhere for a shop, where they could buy souvenirs from Notre Dame. And I was not interested in that at all because I didn't have much money. So, I walked up and found a nice place to sit, because there weren't many people there as yet. And low and behold, in came a young man with the most beautiful little girl. I think she was about three. And she had the sweetest little pinafore on. I just couldn't stop looking at her. I said to the father, "Is this your only child, this little sweetie?"

And he said, "No, I have sons, but my wife has taken them to Steubenville, because they're having a program there. And so, she took the older ones and I have this little one to watch."

And I said, "Well, she's precious. What is her name?"

"Alex," he replied

I said, "Whew!"

So, you see how God works? I was very happy with my little Alex there, and the gentleman. And the talk was beautiful. And then the time when the bus came, we were able to put everything in the bus and we were on our way home.

So now, you see, I've told you stories about angels. And I know there are angels and I hope you do too.

THE ROBE

So, here we go for another vision. The vision was of me, as a little girl, and I know it had to be in Israel. There was grass, maybe about a foot and a half tall, and I was maybe about three years of age, running through the grass. And I was running to this person. I had my little white dress on and blonde hair. And I'm running to this person. He had a long knitted robe on and then the vision ended. I was really amazed.

And then, a few weeks later, as I was coming into church, I kept getting this vision over, and over, and over again, as I'm entering the church. And I said, "Papa God, what's going on?" I was happy with the vision. Why am I getting it over and over again?

Well, when it came time to go to Communion, I went up and I received Jesus. As I came back, and going into the pew, I get another vision. Different. This one now, I'm not three and a half. I must be about six. And I'm standing next to this person, this gentleman, and he's got this same robe on. It's knitted and it's off white. And I'm clinging, hanging on to His robe. And I said, "Wow! I guess I've grown." And I'm holding on to His robe. I said, "How beautiful! Thank you."

And now, as time went on, I don't know how long time passed, but one day, I get another vision. And now I'm about sixteen, and I know it's along the Sea of Galilee 'cuz there's water. It's along the shoreline. And I am skippy-doing it (that's what I call it), skippy-doing it backwards. And who's following me, but that gentleman in that same garment. The knitted garment, off white. And I am so happy, and I'm smiling, and I'm looking at the sandals on His feet.

Do you see what God can do? I was growing, and He was growing with me. He was right along, growing with me, watching me. And I don't know if I told you this, but when I was first Born Again, I was born to take the "Life in the Spirit" seminar, at SS Peter and Paul Church, in Hamburg. I was walking through the parking lot to go into the convent, because that's where we were holding our meetings in the cellar there. A voice spoke to me and said, "Mary, I will teach you myself."

And He certainly has taught me. Now what has He taught me? Love and trust in Him, obedience to Him, and all the wonderful Ten Commandments, for always. We must be as God wants us to be. I'm sure I'm His little girl.

MAX'S FIRST BIRTHDAY

And now, would you believe it? I have another story. I had my dear friend, Anna Martin. She was one of my closest friends because I met her at our church, at that Mission. And we became close friends. Sometimes, she would want to go have her car washed and she'd call me and say, "Mary, you ready to go? I want to go wash my car. I want you to go with me."

I said, "Fine."

Now, we would go with one another wherever the other wanted to go. Well, there was Easter coming up, and I know you've heard of the Divine Mercy Novena. My dear friend, a priest, (who was my son's friend, because my son did some computer work for Father) was having the novena at his parish, which was in the downtown Buffalo area. And so, I said to my dear friend, Annie, "Would you like to go with me? I want to go."

And she said, "Oh, certainly. I'll go with you."

So, we went. We started the novena. Then came the Thursday, and my grandson, Max's, birthday was on Thursday. And I told Anna, I said, "Anna, after the novena, let's go to my son's house, because I've been invited for my little grandson's first birthday."

And she looked at me and said, "I'm not gonna go. If you're going to that birthday party, I'm not gonna go with you."

I said, "Well, ok Sweetie. It's up to you. I'm going."

Well, I got there by myself, and as Mass started, I see something different. It was a real young, nice looking priest. And I noticed the host was not the regular small host. It was a large one. And as he held it up, I see on this host, the head of Christ with the thorns on His head.

I have to tell you that the Polish people, during Christmas time, have something like holy bread. And it's the same consistency of the Eucharist. And it's called oplatek. And in that, are printed pictures of the Christmas Holiday. Jesus in the crib and many other beautiful pictures pressed into these oplateki pieces.

Well, I said, "Whoa! I never knew they would do this to a host." Because, here I see the head of Christ, bent, with the thorns on His head. I thought, "This is something new to me." So when it came time to go up to Communion, a piece of this host was put on my tongue, and as God's witness, I felt a thorn prick my tongue.

I went after the Novena service was over, to my son's house and we celebrated Maxie's first birthday. I think I was really mystified at what I'd seen and gone through at the service.

So, when I could get a chance to talk to our Polish priest, I asked him about this. Do they actually print on the host, like they do on the oplatek, for the Divine Mercy Novena? And he looked at me and he said, "No!"

I said, "Well, Father, this is what I saw. And then when I had a piece put on my tongue, I felt a prick of a thorn."

He said to me, "Oh, he probably just jabbed it into your tongue!"

What do you think?

I said, "Well, Father, what I felt and what I saw, I'm telling you. This is the truth."

So you see, it really amazed me what God can do.

Maybe that's why I'm writing this book – to let you see just what God CAN do. Like as I started the book, there was this young man, and he was mystified with some of these stories I told him. And he pleaded with me, "Please write a book."

So, here I am ready to think I'm finished, but I don't think God is finished.

THE GARMENT

Sunday, as I was going to church, I was asking my Papa God, "Is that the end of these stories?" And bam, bam, bam. He put another one into my mind. So, this one has to do with I think the garment that I've been telling you Jesus has been wearing. For some reason, I feel that He wants you to know about this garment.

So, the years that I spent with my club – they really gave me life. And now I must tell you about some things that weren't so perfect later on. One of my friends, who's still a member of our club, (we're all in our nineties and late eighties), her son, at eighteen, died of cancer. I don't think I was at his funeral, though. Because I think I was gone somewhere. Maybe to my brother in California. I don't know. But I don't remember the funeral, but I do remember the young boy named Joseph. And Joey was so precious. It really tore the hearts out of all of us, because of his sweetness, and he was so beautiful. Such a wonderful, wonderful young man.

So, then, later on now, time is going on, and we all had children. To all of our children, we all were Aunties and Uncles, even though we weren't related to any. The children always called me Aunt Mary and Uncle Leo (this was my husband). So, it was really a huge beautiful family. We would have picnics out at Como Park and different parks. For the kids, we had our little Mary Banasiak, who would always have games and prizes for all the children. We were all bound together. This was God's love for all of us.

So, then, one of the boys, Ronnie, now a young man, was driving his car and he felt ill. So, he pulled the car over off the road, and he had a severe stroke. This really hurt the hearts of all of us, because Ronnie, too, (all of our children were beautiful), he was always willing to help anyone. He helped his Momma and Dad. He helped every one that needed him.

Well, Ronnie passed on, and here's what I think God wants you to know. At the funeral. At the cemetery, it was a beautiful day. I remember the sun was out. So as we're all outside talking… sad. I got a vision. And this vision was as real as life could be. Here was Ronnie, in this same garment – a knitted, off white. And he was looking up and the smile on his face was so beautiful. I said, "Thank you, Papa God." Just to see that look on his face.

I think something in these stories is about this garment. Every time I saw a person in my visions, this garment is what they have on. So, what this means, I really don't know. But, it's just amazing what God can do if you but give him your life. And that's what I did with my Papa God.

SERVANT

My life was over when my husband was gone. The children would all leave the house. And I told my Papa God, "God, I don't know what to do with my life. I give it to you." And he took it. But you see, when He took it, I also became His servant. Someone that He could call upon. Because, in the scriptures, it says, "The fields are ripe, but I have no workers." And I ask you, do you want to be a worker? But, you must be ready. Because when you become His worker, you become someone that is just different than the rest of the world. It is not you who does the work for our God. It is the Holy Spirit that lives in you. God becomes so happy because His love can be spread among his children. If we don't have this love of Christ in us, we become like salt that loses its flavor. Many people have asked me why I smile so much. I tell them it's because I know the Master. Just last Thursday, when I received Jesus at Communion, the host was so sweet, and do you know I wouldn't stop smiling all day. I'm driving my car and I'm smiling. What a day full of joy and love. And what empowers you is love. His love just fills you because, you see, we can talk to people. But, if we don't have that love of Christ in us…

That love comes from the Holy Spirit. And we must be filled to the brim. Because, then that Spirit will overflow into people around you. And that's what's so beautiful.

ROSES

Well, guess what? I went to my Legion of Mary meeting tonight, and while we were talking, two of the ladies told them how they took flowers to a senior citizen elderly nursing home. When they said "flowers", a light went on in my head. So, I have to tell you of this story of flowers.

Whenever I was asked to give a talk, I always went to Papa God. I would ask Him for help. He never let me down. This time, when I was to give a talk at a Charismatic meeting at a church, this is what I did. This time, He told me to take two roses. One very, very closed up tight, and another rose, fully wide opened. This I did and that was where it all started.

As I started the speech, I asked the people, "What kind of a rose are you … are we? Do we know our God? Are we all uptight? Just never to speak out the word to people we meet? You cannot smell the fragrance of a very tight closed rose. Whereas the wide open rose, you can smell the beauty and fragrance of the rose. Now this fragrance is the Word of God."

Of course, I went on and on with the beauty of the rose. You see what God can do? Wow!

A KNEE

Another story… I wasn't feeling well. I went to my doctor and I told him I felt strange on the left side of my abdomen. He says, "Well, we'll send you in for a MRI."

I said, "Well, I just had one cataract removed on my left eye, and I'm gonna have the right one done."

"Well," he says. "Cancel this second appointment."

And I said, "No. I'm not going to cancel because I want to get these eyes done."

He said, "Ok."

So, my plan was to get to the eye doctor to have the other cataract removed. I had to spend the night with my son and his wife, in West Seneca, because my daughter-in-law was going to take me in to have the cataract removed and she would be there to bring me home. Plus, I had to go for the MRI. So I said, "We can do it. I'll have the eye done, then we'll go for the MRI."

So, I had the eye done. And my daughter-in-law, Gracie, she's so sweet. Everybody should have a Gracie. She took me and we went and had the MRI. Well, of course, I had to wait to see if it came out alright. But, to our surprise, the surgeon came out and said, "You're not going anywhere. You are going under surgery at noontime."

So, I went under surgery. They took two thirds of my colon out. I had cancer in the colon – a huge one. And even my children saw it, the surgeon allowed my children to see it. They told me it looked horrible. But, he told the children he was quite sure he got all the cancer. Because he looked me over real good inside.

And so, I'm now in the hospital for a week, and then I go to Garden Gate, which is run by the McGuire Group, and my daughter works there. She saw to it that I got there, so as she could come visit me easily. So, I'm there, and I have a real bad back. I have three compound fractures of the spine. And their way of helping people is to put you in a wheelchair and let you sit in the wheelchair.

Well, it just so happened that when I'm in a wheelchair, my back just kills me. So, when they take me for breakfast, I said, "Take me in a hurry." And then I would just gobble down my oatmeal, and I would push myself back to my room, in hopes that somebody would take me out of the wheelchair and put me in the bed. Then the pain wasn't so bad.

So, one day, this nurse (see how nasty I can be) – I said to her, "Do you run a torture chamber here?"

And she looked at me, so surprised to hear this coming out of me. She said, "No!"

I said, "Well, if you keep me in these wheelchairs, I'm in a torture chamber."

She said, "Well, we'll get you pain pills." Wrong choice!

Would you believe it, I took the pain pills and I lost all of my appetite. I could not even look at food. If I saw hamburgers on television, I just couldn't stand it! And my children were trying to bring me something that would give me joy to eat. And even then, I didn't want to eat. It was just terrible what I got from those pills.

So, they right away decide I had to have physical therapy. Well, after you've had your insides all cut up, and your back is killing you, they want me to have therapy. So, I have to do what they tell me. Well, they would take me in this wheelchair, which was torture to start with. Then we would go, and they had a room where everybody got their therapy. They had two big beds there, and they had leather over the top of them. And I pleaded with the girl, "Just let me do my exercises while lying down." I can kick my feet. I can move my hands. But I could not sit straight up.

And she was sweet. She said, "Fine. Good."

So, that was the way I did my exercises. Well, now here's where the story gets interesting.

One day, they put me on the other bed, not the one I was usually on. And a gentleman comes in and he lays on the opposite bed, close to me. There's maybe about a foot and a half of room between us. The physical therapist was a tall, strong looking man, and he was working on this gentleman's knee.

All of a sudden, to me the Lord says, "Mary, pray over that man's knee."

So I tell the physical therapist, "I think God wants me to pray over this man's knee."

He says, "Well, don't ask me. Ask the man."

So, I said, "Fine. Gentleman, would you like me to pray over your knee?"

He said, "Miss, I'll take anything you can give me." Because he was suffering with that knee, alot.

So, they got me up. I believe they pulled the wheelchair over and I sat in that. And I put my hands on this gentleman's knee and prayed. How I prayed, I don't remember. Then I went back on my bed. As this gentleman left, the physical therapist turned to me, and he said, "Do you think I can come up to your room and talk to you?"

I said, "Fine."

And twice he came to my room and we talked about Jesus. So, I kind of think, you see, the whole think wasn't for the knee. It was about the physical therapist. God's work again. What a God! He even could use me when I was half alive. My Rosemary said to me one day, "Now you know why you're here, Mom." God needs us so his love can reach all of his children.

A NURSE

Now more stories go on. Even though I was not in good shape, Papa God needed me where I was. And this day, my dear friend who started my journey with me, Dan Gallagher, (his son is helping me write this book), he came to visit me. And in came a nurse. She was so uptight. So distraught. Dan said to me, "What is this woman doing here? These are sick people. She shouldn't be working here."

Well, he went home and later in the evening my daughter, Rosemary, came in to see me. She worked just a few rooms away. And in came the nurse. And so angry. And yells out loud, "I'm gonna get a divorce." When I heard that and I looked at this poor soul, who was suffering terribly.

I said, "Honey, please come and sit next to me." And she did. And I called my daughter, Rosemary, over, and I said we're gonna pray over her. Well, I first said my little prayer that I always say before touching anybody. And then the two of us prayed over her. And you won't believe this. She melted like a marshmallow before the fire. Tears were just flowing down her cheeks and flowing and flowing. You could just see the hurt that was so heavy in this poor woman. And God, through His love, had touched her.

And that's why it's so important, people, to know your Father God. To know the Holy Spirit. Because there's so many people that are hurting so. And as we laid hands and prayed over her, God's love just filled her, and gave her new life. And after that night, many times I would see her, and she had a joyous smile on her face. She was living a new life. Whether she ever divorced the man, I don't know. But, I know her heart was changed. And it was not me. And it was not Rosemary. It was our Papa God. And He knows so many people are hurting. And he seems to give me that knowledge now.

THE TAILOR

Well, I was sure I finished my last chapter in this book, but then I had to go to Feel Rite store and pick up these pills I needed, and on the way there, I started to think of my friends, Joe and Josephine. Joe is a tailor. He has his own tailor shop in Hamburg – the town I was going to be going to. I picked up my pills, and as I started to get back on the road, I really had a strong feeling that I must go see my two friends. This was such a strong feeling, I knew I must go and see them.

When I arrived by their store and home, I was happy to see there weren't a lot of cars in his parking lot. This meant we could have a little time to talk. Joe told Josephine, his wife, I had come, because he caught the tail end of my car pulling in. Josephine told him he was wrong. But, when I opened the door, Josephine was right there. She was really looking to see if I had come. Well, of course, now the hugs and kisses started.

I hadn't seen either one of them since they came to the hospital to see me after I had my surgery. That was nine months ago. I remember that visit because my sons were in the room visiting with me when they came in. You would have thought Joe was another son because they all had such a wonderful visit together.

Now, why this visit. This was really the work of the Holy Spirit. You see, every time I have ever stopped in to visit them, they were in some kind of a big, unhappy dilemma. Once it had to do with her daughter, the next time with their son, and once with the illness of a very close relative. This time it was over Joe. It was about our Joe. He really wasn't feeling well at all. And here he had a shop just chuck full of work. This is the time of proms and weddings. Josephine was being worked so hard, too, because Joe needed help.

They just couldn't believe I had come to them. You see, during all these visits the other times, I was there to lead us in prayer for these people. And Joe knew how strong prayer can be and how it always helps so much. Josephine and I laid hands on our Joe and we had our beautiful prayer time. The Holy Spirit would always take over and send me to them when this time was needed.

What a beautiful day. You see, this same morning, after Mass, a lovely, lovely lady would not let me leave the church. She told me I must pray over her. She had just found out that she had some problem with her heart. She told me if I could survive the surgery I had, and now be driving a car and coming to church, I was the one she wanted to have pray over her. Well, my friend and I did pray over her. Now, why am I telling you all this? It is because our Papa God knows who needs Him. And the best way for Papa to help them is to see this strong faith in Him. When they listen to His Spirit, they do ask for prayer. Believe me, Papa God is in control. So, always listen to His Spirit when He talks to you.

YOUR SPECIAL SOMEONE

I just was in my neighboring church. And after mass, this young woman was just sitting there, head hanging, and looking so lost. So, I went over to her and I said, "You know, Honey, I think you need a hug." And I hugged her and kissed her on the forehead. And later, when I was getting into my car, she came to me. She said, "You'll never know how I needed that hug at that moment."

So, now the stories are over, I think … unless God sends me another one. There have been so many of them. But you know, it's all worthwhile. I'm eighty-seven. Soon, I'll be going to see the Boss. But, isn't it wonderful? He says that there's two lives in the Son (Sun) – one to live here, and His Son gives us eternal life. That is such a big, big step, when you realize what love this God has for us humans on this earth. And we are His children. He's shown me I am His little girl. And you're His little girl and little boy. But all it takes is just to open your heart. And you know people say you gotta ask Him in. I never ask. I gave. I gave Him my whole life. And He took it. And He knows your heart. He knows where your heart is.

Take this to heart ... Then Jesus told them another story: "The kingdom of heaven is like a man who planted good seed in his field. That night, when everyone was asleep, his enemy came and planted weeds among the wheat and then left. Later, the wheat sprouted and the heads of grain grew, but the weeds also grew. Then the man's servants came to him and said, 'You planted good seed in your field. Where did the weeds come from?' The man answered, 'An enemy planted weeds.' The servants asked, 'Do you want us to pull up the weeds?' The man answered, 'No, because when you pull up the weeds, you might also pull up the wheat. Let the weeds and the wheat grow together until the harvest time. At harvest time I will tell the workers, "First gather the weeds and tie them together to be burned. Then gather the wheat and bring it to my barn."   Matthew 13:24-30

What seed are you? Will you be the good seed? So take heed my little one that's reading this book. Take time. I always tell my son this – go sit outside or somewhere where it's real quiet. Nobody around you. Nothing around you. And just quietly talk to your Creator. Ask Him to show you what it's all about – this life. And I grant you, as I'm sitting here talking, He will show you. And if His love fills you, you'll know a new life like I know one now. I have to love all. My Jesus says love your enemy. I preach to people in need. Please, I just told someone the other day, "You know, don't carry hatred around. Because if you hate, you're not hurting that person. You're hurting yourself. And no one needs that hurt."

So listen to a little old lady, who's been there from the beginning of life – so alone, broken home, but always knowing that God, not God because I didn't know God, but I knew there was someone special, someone very special that was with me and taught me, and stood by my side. And I'm sure you'll find that special person, too.

God bless all of you. And I have to thank my wonderful Cory, and this wonderful lady that's sitting across from me right now. Sweet, loving people for helping me on this journey. Because life is a journey and if we take it, and we take the right road, we'll find a beautiful, beautiful journey. You will have troubles. I had troubles. But you know, He's with you all the time, and He will give you strength, and love, and the courage to face it all. God bless you. Keep love in your heart and a smile on your face. The great secret of life. Jesus will show you the way. His Papa has watched me all my life and He will do the same for you. Trust this little old lady. Mary is her name.

By writing this little book, I pray that whoever reads about God's work will be able to really know our wonderful Father God and also how much He loves His children. Look where I came from. I never knew there was a God. But, I knew in my heart there was someone very special that gave me the beauty of life that was all around me. Are your eyes open to see? Are your ears open to hear? As I have said to my children, go sit somewhere and just be still and be quiet. Ask God to show you where He is real. He will never fail you. You are His and He loves you so much.

Now, as I close this book for sure, all I can say is – I pray you will listen and keep asking, keep speaking to your Father God, and remember His Spirit is here waiting to hear from you. God Bless all of you who read this book. I wrote it for Papa God, so His little ones will really learn about Him and His Mother. This wonderful Holy Family of ours wait for you. Please don't let this Heavenly Family down. OK? ….

Love you - Mary

ABOUT THE AUTHOR

Mary was born and raised in California. She always knew there was a "Very Special Someone" in her life. She met and married her Leo and together they raised five children. Mary now resides in Western New York where she enjoys nature and continues her work for her Papa God.

Made in the USA
Charleston, SC
28 July 2014